10/14/02

MORRISVILLE:

A Native Hidden Community

MORRISVILLE:

A Native Hidden Community

Nemattanew
(Chief Roy Crazy Horse)

Powhatan Press - Rancocas, New Jersey

Powhatan Press
P.O. Box 225
Rankokus Indian Reservation
Rancocas Road
Rancocas, NJ 08073

Published by Powhatan Press under the direction of the Powhatan Renape Nation

Printed in the United States of America

Library of Congress Control Number: 2002104951

ISBN: 0-9719465-0-7

www.powhatan.org

"We Don't Have Much, but We Have Each Other."

Acknowledgments

Sharing has been a fundamental principle of our people.
In hard times, this has kept us united as a nation.

Our people have shared once again by opening their family albums
to make treasured photographs available for this book.

On behalf of the Powhatan Renape Nation, I extend to each of them
our warm thanks for sharing their memories with us.

Kathryn Samuels Anderson	Shirley M. Hunter
Nathaniel Beasley	Chief Roy Crazy Horse
Lavern Cattlett Benson	Maxine Jones
Howard Carney	Geraldine Carney King
Orville Carney	Doloris Hunter Maddox
Ruby Carney	Carl Major
Carey Chandler	Lillian Bundy Mosley
Sid Custalow	Powhatan Renape Nation
Juanita Bundy Davis	Gilbert Samuels
Gladys Harmon Doe	Vergie Byrd Unis
Charles Games	Doris Johnson Willis
Lorraine Parker Greene	Elaine Wright
Gladys Carney Harmon	Theresa Cox Wyche
Kim T. Hunter	St. Matthew's Methodist Church

This book would not have been possible without the kind support of so many people who came forward with assistance, encouragement, and advice, and we are sincerely grateful. All of you have helped the Powhatan Renape Nation take its place among its New Jersey neighbors.

I give a special thank you to Burlington County College, for their generous contribution in the production of this book.

– Chief Roy Crazy Horse

This history is dedicated to the Powhatan Renape Nation of the past.
Our ancestors struggled against desperate odds and survived
so we would have a place to build our Nation.

This history is dedicated to the Powhatan Renape Nation of the
present, our people, our relatives, who have built a Nation on
the foundation made by our ancestors.

This history is dedicated to the Powhatan Renape Nation of the
future, our children, grandchildren, to the generation yet unborn.
May you prosper and remain united in the Nation which has been
prepared for you with sacrifice, work, care, and much love.

Contents

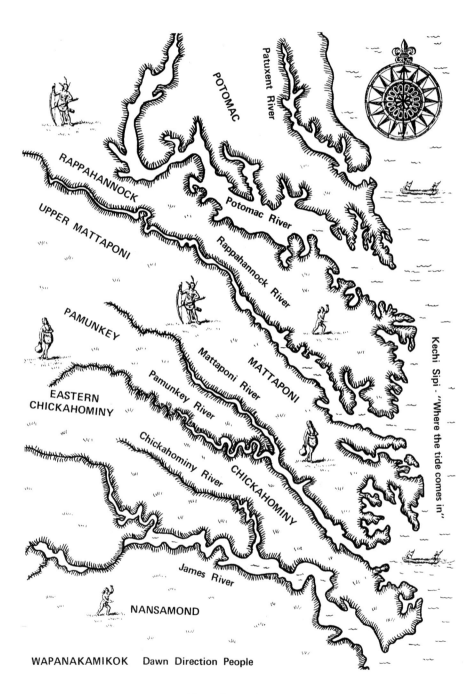

POTOMAC

Patuxent River

Potomac River

RAPPAHANNOCK

UPPER MATTAPONI

Rappahannock River

PAMUNKEY

MATTAPONI

Mattaponi River

EASTERN CHICKAHOMINY

Pamunkey River

Chickahominy River

CHICKAHOMINY

James River

NANSAMOND

Kechi Sipi - "Where the tide comes in"

WAPANAKAMIKOK   Dawn Direction People

Tidewater area of Virginia: Birthplace of the Powhatan Tribes

IV

The Powhatan Renape Nation: The Foundation Of The Morrisville Community

Before Europeans came to North America, the Powhatan Nation lived a rich life in our traditional territories along the Atlantic coastal "Tidewater" areas south of Manhattan Island to what is now the Virginia-North Carolina border. We had over 200 villages in our territory, which extended along the rivers westward from the Atlantic Ocean to the point where river navigation was impossible. We called this area *Tsenacomacoh.*

Our culture was shaped by the river/bay environment, which provided communication and trade routes, fish and birds for food, rich riverbank soil for agriculture. Game was hunted in the higher elevations. The forests provided nuts and berries, as well as fuel and materials for shelter. We traded with our neighbors in the Delaware River area.

When the English arrived in the early 1600s, we extended cautious friendship, but as the English attempted to dominate the area, there was strong resistance. The English negotiated treaties, broke them, and then wanted to negotiate again. When the English settlers and tobacco planters flood-

 1

ed Tsenacomacoh, oppressive racist laws were passed to facilitate our division, relocation, and displacement. Our nation became refugees in their own lands. In many cases, our people were taken into slavery.

Despite these adversities, our sense of community and identity as a people remained intact. Indeed, they were strengthened. We had to adopt a very special strategy for survival.

Moving On: A Survival Strategy

One strategy was to move to other lands. Many of the Rappahanock people, in particular, moved northward in the Tidewater area. As their areas were encroached upon, individual Powhatan families drifted off to more promising areas. Gradually, other Powhatan families would join them. They would grow and prosper and consolidate, after which pressures or lack of opportunity for continuing consolidation would cause individual families to drift off to set the same cycle once again. Relocation to more favorable environments enhanced survival. In this way, we escaped the ethnic and racial prejudices of the slave-based South.

Still, there were dangers. Racist laws permitted only two legal racial categories: blacks and whites. We had become invisible as a people. We were denied all civil rights. However, we continued to survive as a people.

By 1800, most Powhatan people were Christians. Publicly, we looked "assimilated." Privately, we remained Powhatans. We were also able to "fit in" because many of our rural neighbors had adapted our own economic strategies. We could continue to hunt and fish and survive.

In order to maintain our Indian identity, young men and women sought spouses amongst other Tidewater Indian communities in other areas of Virginia and along the Atlantic coast. Strict policies regarding inter-marriage were practiced as part of retaining Indian identity.

Also, migration continued. A group of Pamunkeys and Chickahominies left Virginia for a journey to a destination, which today is not known. Their fate remains a mystery.

During the Civil War, many of our men joined the Union service as sol-diers, guides, or seamen, while some fled to Canada to avoid conscription in the confederate service. After the war, repressive racial discrimination intensified.

At the dawn of the 20th Century, among our people, only the Pamunkey and Mattaponi had managed to have any part of their original territory in Tidewater Virginia reserved. However, at least ten groups still survived somewhere near their homelands. Among these were the Rappahannocks of Caroline, Essex, and King and Queen Counties. Three centuries of sur-vival, three major wars with Europeans, but surviving still.

Why did we want to call ourselves Indians and make life so hard for our-selves in biracial Virginia? Few people understood that for Indian people, Indian identity is an extremely precious thing, something to be clung to, no matter the pressure against it.

(left to right) Opitchipan Major, Powhatan Major, Sarah Langston Major, Nanecow Major, Lee Major on the Mattapony Reservation, VA

The Powhatans and the Nanticokes

One of the peoples with whom the Powhatan people had contact were the Nanticokes who lived in the region of what today is Sussex County, Delaware. They too had formed a coherent community and a survival strategy, which included migration and intermarriage with other Indian people. The principal families included the Carneys, Cokers, Johnsons, Mosleys, Reeds, Ridgeways, Sammons and Wrights. In about 1865, a group of Nanticokes took up residence in Blackwood Town, in what today is Camden County.

Not long after, Powhatans from Virginia also discovered that New Jersey was indeed a promising area for migration. Industrialization and expanding urban area offered employment and a less racist environment. The migration northward tended to concentrate in the Philadelphia/Camden area. The New Jersey side of the Delaware River, an area of what today is Pennsauken Township, provided a riverside environment off the beaten track, which seemed familiar, safe, and comfortable. Morrisville – named after John Morris and now considered a part of Delair or East Delair, as it is sometimes called – was located within a half mile of Fish House Cove and a small community called "Fish House" on the Delaware River just north of Petty's Island. Camden was still a small town in the 1870s and 1880s.

Along the Delaware and the creeks which flowed into it, there was land for hunting, gathering of medicines and country food, gardening and fishing. The Cove and the nearby Cooper River and Pochack Creek, flowing along the north side of Morrisville, were well stocked with a variety of fish. Ducks and geese were abundant, as well as turtles, eels, blue crabs, and crayfish. There were muskrat, raccoons, rabbits, squirrels, and opossum. The area was also known for its artesian wells and sources of pure water.

For both Nanticoke and Powhatan, the survival strategies, which have served them well in Delaware and Virginia, were again employed: Seek a community of mixed racial identity. Let a few families locate, more move in, consolidate. Keep a low profile. Be proud of being an Indian, but don't tell anyone. Find other Indians for spouses to maintain identity. Get along with neighbors, cooperate – but remain separate.

Adolphus Johnson (1898-1949)

Ora Beasley Johnson (1906-1993)

Robert Plume

Sallie Acrey Fortune Steele (1906-1999)

Harry Wright

Helen Reed Wright

Jacob Mosley

Roy and Dell Crazy Horse

Pearl Mosley Bundy

Morrisville: A Familiar Destination
Never Before Seen

Morrisville was the oldest settlements of what is today Pennsauken Township. The first settler was William Harvey, who came in the early 1700s. Many of the early settlers of Morrisville were part Black/part Mohican. They had a small community of "free people of color" centered on the home of William and Levina Pratt. It was an ideal place for Powhatans and Nanticokes to conceal themselves, raise their children – and survive.

Sometime in the mid-1860s, Nehemiah and Sarah (Sammons) Carney moved to the area, and established their homestead in Morrisville.

It was natural that Nehemiah Carney would join with neighbor William Luff, who had married Victoria Pratt, to found a church. In October 1867, a Wesleyan Methodist Church was organized in Morrisville. It became known as "St. Matthew's Church," and it became the focal point of the Powhatan Renape community. Later, a separate Bethel A.M.E. Church was built near the present site of St. Matthew's Church. (The building was later moved to Haddonfield Road, and known as the Jordan town Church.)

13

St. Matthew's Church, circa 1867

St. Matthew's Church, 2001

Nehemiah and Sarah's son Robert was born in Morrisville in 1873. Dan Carney was born in 1877. Henry Carney joined the community.

In 1881, Delair – today lying on the west and north side of Morrisville – was founded as a resort for wealthy families from the city of Philadelphia.

On June 10, 1882, Nehemiah Carney purchased a lot adjoining the Wesleyan Methodist Church lot on the east side of today's Pleasant Avenue in Morrisville. He and two sons James and George, worked at Hatch's Fairview Brickyard located on Fish House Cove. Still more Nanticokes has moved into the area: Frank Harmon, Mary Parker, and Frank Miller.

In 1883 Stockton Township was renamed "Pennsauken Township."

In 1890 William Bundy, who lived next door to Lee Acrey and his wife Nora Byrd in Rappahannock country in Virginia, came to Morrisville and married Nehemiah Carney's daughter Emma.

In 1885, the Pennsylvania Railway opened a bridge across the Delaware River connecting Pennsauken Township with northeast Philadelphia. A station was opened at Delair, but little was changed. There was little population growth, and the Hatch Brickyard was the only industry. The only transformation was agricultural – new farmland, and peach and pear orchards.

Charles Mosley, Sr.'s car, circa 1920   Nehemiah and Sarah Carney's house (rear of photo)

Ethel Mosley Carney

Lee Acrey (1861-1910)

Nora Byrd Acrey (1873-1934)

Emma Carney Bundy (1881-1968)

Ida Carney Still (1869-1934)

George Carney (1864-1898)

Daniel Carney (1877-1940)

Morrisville in the 20th Century

By 1900, John Carney was living in his father's household with his wife Maggie Still. Dan Carney and his wife Pearlie were also living with Nehemiah and Sarah. On the same lot, but in a separate house, Amelia, the widowed wife of George Carney, was living with her six children, the youngest age 2, the oldest 13 – Nehemiah and Sarah's grandchildren. Amelia was working as a washerwoman, and 13-year-old William was a working man – he would later be known as "Uncle Greenie." Henry Carney lived nearby with his daughter Ella and her three children. Next door was William Bundy and Emma Carney and their three children. Other neighbors were Robert and Mary Carney and their two children, and Charles and Ida (Ridgeway) Carney and their two children. Still all six families owned their own homes – Nehemiah Carney was a fine carpenter, and he trained his sons and sons-in-law well. This reinforced the self-sufficiency and pride of the community.

With the planting of those first seeds, the Powhatan Renape Nation began to consolidate decade by decade as the industrial revolution offered new

William Bundy (1888 - 1957) and Emma Carney Bundy (1881-1968)

Robert Carney (1874-1967) and
Mary Cortney Carney (1882-1960)

Charles Carney (1878-1948)

opportunities and liberties in the Camden/Philadelphia area. The same skills of social interaction, which permitted the Powhatan people to survive amidst the racism of Virginia, would again serve them well. The Powhatans arrival in the Morrisville area would fit in with the Nanticoke intermarriage policies.

For both people, the site, which would nurture them in New Jersey, offered the right conditions: the opportunity to integrate with their neighbors while maintaining their separateness and their identity. There they would continue to do as they had done in the past: put down roots, bring in new members, consolidate the community.

Eugene Bundy with nieces Dorothy and Betty Bundy

Al Bundy (1888-1956) and John Carney (1912-1947)

Maintaining Identity

Later, as the Morrisville community consolidated, it maintained its internal controls with its own leaders, among them, Dan Carney. While they consistently recognized themselves as Indians, and demonstrated their identity by seeing to it that their children generally married Indians, they didn't advertise that fact to the surrounding community – their Virginia experience had taught them this was neither necessary nor advisable for their survival. Besides, their relatives in Virginia recognized them and continued to migrate northwards to live with them. This fit the general pattern found in the Virginia communities: a move is made, roots are put down deeper and people then have a place where they can live, raise their families, and die in the same location, their places taken by their children.

Survival in Morrisville meant suffering discrimination as a community. Although Morrisville was well established as an eight-block community, it was the last in Pennsauken to have electricity. It was the last in Pennsauken to have water – Morrisville residents hauled their water in a wheelbarrow from a common well. Morrisville residents were the last in Pennsauken to

25

Sidney, Ella, Arlayne Custalow

Linese Miller Marvin

Lee Major, Elston Opecouchana Major,
Carl Opechancanough Major

Laverne, Edward, Fayette Carney Catlett

Ida Carney Parker and Nathaniel Parker

Susan Acree Bundy and Clarence Bundy

Ruth Acree Chandler, James Chandler, and Cary Chandler

Rosa Johnson Beasley

Anna Schmidt Johnson (1888-1968)

Felsher Beasley

Ida and Mordecai Byrd

have sidewalks. Morrisville children had to cross what was then one of New Jersey's busiest highways in order to go to and from the two room second class Union School with its pot bellied stove and outhouses. Indians were not permitted in the white school just a few blocks away from Morrisville.

The Morrisville community continued to grow with the arrival of more people from Delaware and Virginia. Not all lived right in Morrisville, but Morrisville was the social, church and activity center – the heartbeat of the people. Their names were our names: Acree, Adams, Beasley, Bradby, Bundy, Byrd, Catlett, Fortune, Harmon, Hunter, Johnson, Major, Miller, Parker, Wright and Custalow. The Custalows and Majors came up from the Mattaponi Reservation in Virginia. Lewitt and Estelle (Henshaw) Adams also came from the Mattaponi Reservation to Philadelphia, but they soon found the Morrisville community and affiliated it. Kenova Bradby did the same – his parents were indentified as "full blood Indians" during a special census of the Chickahominy Tribe, and Kenova's uncle, Edward Pemberton Bradby, was Eastern Chickahominy Chief from 1924 into the 1940's.

Between 1900 and 1910, Daniel Carney formed his own household with his wife Pearl. His brother Edward lived with them. As did his nephew Howard Carney and Howard's wife Ethel. Horace Sammons came over from the Delaware to join the household with his wife Mary – they had seven children. About this time, Baldwin Bundy moved to New Jersey from the Rappahannock community in Essex County, Virginia. His son, Robert Bundy married George Carney's daughter Lillian and established their home on

Morrisville Road next door to Charles and Ida Carney and their five children, and William and Emma Bundy and their seven. Lee Major and his family moved to Morrisville from the West Point Reservation in Virginia.

Bertha Carney Chandler Games

Clarence Bundy and Ida Miller Bundy

(Left to Right) Etta Bundy Samuels, Cornelia Bundy Cox, Clarence Bundy, Emma Carney Bundy, Ida Bundy Miller

Joseph Bundy and Daniel Bundy

Eugene Bundy

Lillian Carney Bundy

Howard Carney

Robert Bundy

Morrisville Begins to Develop

At the beginning of World War I, in 1914, the Pleasantville Land Company filed a plot survey to develop two more streets north of Pleasant Avenue in Morrisville. The plan was for 135 lots, each 20 feet wide, along Tripoli and Romeo Avenues off Derousse Avenue. At the same time, more Powhatan Renape people were arriving. Clarence Hunter, Sr. arrived from Virginia and married Mary Carney. He bought two of the lots.

By 1920, Morrisville had at least 15 households, including William and Amanda Hunter, William and Emma Bundy and their daughter Etta and her husband William Samuels, William and Pauline Bundy, Robert and Lillian Bundy, Clarence and Mary Hunter, Charles and Ida Carney, George and Pearl Bundy, Daniel and Pearlie Carney, Amelia Carney, Howard and Ethel Carney, Albert and Clara Bundy, and Baldwin and Artie Bundy. The population of Morrisville was 61.

The Rappahannock, Chickahominy, Nansamund and Mattaponi, together with the Nanticoke of Delaware, reorganized in 1923 as the "Powhatan

Chief Black Hawk (1885-1980)

Confederacy." A Virginia-born leader rose up to provide liaison to all Powhatan peoples in the Delaware Valley area and into New England. He was Chief Black Hawk (1885-1980), selected in the 1920's during an assembly of Powhatan peoples as "field chief" for the Powhatans living away from the homelands.

About the same time, 1924, Nehemiah and Sarah Carney passed on. Nehemiah left no will, and his property was divided among 24 living descendants: Ida Carney who married Charles Still, Robert Carney who married Mary Courtney, John Carney who married Maggie Still, Daniel Carney who married Pearl Banks, and Emma Carney who married William Bundy. There were also grandchildren, the sons and daughters of George (who died about 1900): William "Uncle Greenie" Carney who had married Sadie Broadnax; Howard Carney who had married Ethel Mosley, the daughter of Isaiah Mosley (also a Delaware Nanticoke); Lillian Carney who had married Robert Bundy and Mary Carney who had married Clarence Hunter. Harry Carney's sons, Harry and Howard, also shared in the property.

One of the memorable residents of Morrisville was "Chief" Norman Carney, the eldest of Robert and Mary Carney's fourteen children. He went to school until the third grade, when he had to leave to labor in the Soap Works to help support the family. The History of Pennsauken Historical Society in 1966 notes that Norman was not about to hide the Indian heritage he had acquired from his parents.

Clara Pride Bundy with daughters Jean and Fran Bundy

Pearl Banks Carney

Harry Carney (1891-1918) and Baldwin Bundy (b.1888)

Etta Bundy Samuels and William Samuels

Mary Carney Hunter

Amanda Carney Hunter

William Carney

"Chief" Norman Carney

Bernice Carney Comfort

Dorothy Carney Hunter

Gladys Carney Harmon

Claudia Carney Collins, Gilbert Catlett, Joyce Cattlet, Fayetta Carney Cattlet, Octavia Carney Collins

Octavia Carney Collins, Gladys Carney Harmon, Claudia Carney Collins, Bernice Carney Comfort

Orville Carney

Harold Carney

Elmer Carney

Clem Carney

Consolidation and Economic Progress

Throughout the 1920's, the Powhatan Renape community continued to consolidate. William and Emma Bundy bought two lots on Lumby (now Forrest) Avenue. Daniel Carney bought two lots on Tripoli Avenue, while Clarence and William Hunter bought three lots on the same street. Robert and Lillian Bundy bought two lots in the Columbia Grove portion of Tripoli Avenue. Double lots were popular: there was room for a garden, even a few pigs.

On December 3, 1924, Nehemiah Bundy – Nehemiah Carney's grandson who had married Louise Parker of Virginia – purchased Nehemiah Carney's original lot next to St. Matthew's Church. There they owned a store in partnership with Bernice Carney Comfort. Nehemiah and his family lived above what the community called "The Bundy Store." Other business people included Harold Carney and his barbershop, George Bundy's "Hillsdale Poolroom."

There was also the "fish plant" business. The Morrisville people used their entrepreneurial skills to gather, clean, pack and market a local aquatic plant considered a weed for householders to use in their aquariums.

The biggest local business, however, was the Drew Drop Inn on the corner of Derousse Avenue and Burlington Pike. It had been purchased by Clarence Hunter and his wife Mary (Carney) in 1936. Hunter and his children – Clarence Jr., Norris, Claude and Alma – owned and operated this popular nightspot for 42 years until it closed in 1979.

Customers drove all the way from Philadelphia to hear the musicians the Hunter's brought in – Dizzy Gillespie, Pearl Bailey, Clark Terry, McCoy Tyner, Elvin Jones and John Coltrane. The Dew Drop Inn employed many local people as cooks and waiters – one of the few places where the Powhatan people could work. As they had done for so long, during the Great Depression, the people of Morrisville did what they did best: survived, largely invisible and unnoticed by outsiders. City directories just passed it by. Maps were published – but Morrisville was rarely mentioned. When New Jersey's cemeteries were surveyed, the Morrisville cemetery was left out, although it is the oldest cemetery in Pennsauken Township.

The Powhatan Renape people shared food and resources, and worked together. The Dew Drop Inn, the fish plant business, fishing, hunting and gardening made survival possible. Because Morrisville did not have electricity until the late 1930's, residents dug storage pits and cut ice from the river for summer use.

As one Powhatan Renape elder puts it, "I'm going to tell you how we survived – by working together, if one had, we all had. Nobody would go to bed without his or her stomach being full."

Dew Drop Inn - Local Night Club (1936-1979)

Community Members Working at the Fish Plant

First row: Etta Carney, Pauline Cooper Carney, Howard Carney
Second row: Mary Hunter
Third row: Ida Still, Lillian Bundy, Emma Mosley

We Kept Getting Stronger: Post-World War II

World War II brought jobs. Powhatan Renape people helped in the New York Shipyard in Camden. However, prejudice against Morrisville continued to isolate the community. Houses were not connected to a sewer system until 1953. Streets remained unpaved until the 1960's, long after neighboring Delair's streets had been paved.

After World War II, there was a push for industrial development of Pennsauken Township. Gilbert Samuels and some other men founded the Mohegan Rod and Gun Club in 1954, on eight acres of land in Tabernacle, New Jersey, near the Pine Barrens. As has been Powhatan Renape culture for centuries, they often brought home "feeds" for the entire tribe.

In 1962, the Powhatan Renape Nation "went public" for the first time by opening an office in Philadelphia at 4th and Girard. Our office there had a toll-free number so the people in Morrisville could call the office. La Donna Harris, then head of "American Indians for Opportunity" and a vice-presi-

49

La Donna Harris with Roy Crazy Horse, Charles Juancito, and Community Members in front of Powhatan Office on 4th and Girard in Philadelphia, PA - Circa 1972.

Mohegan Rod Gun Club - Circa 1951

dential candidate, visited us. Roy Crazy Horse was elected to the Board of Directors of the Philadelphia District Indian Education in 1963, charged with responsibility for policy-making and planning for Indian children in New Jersey and Pennsylvania. Our newsletter, *Attan Akamik,* was published in 1968. When Leon Shenandoah was unjustly tried in Philadelphia, our people coordinated lodging and food for over 300 Indians who came to Philadelphia to join us in demonstrating about this tragedy.

In 1972, when the Powhatan Renape Nation took on a legal personality, the leadership which Roy Crazy Horse had provided prior to that time was formalized with his selection as Chief (Chief Black Hawk died in 1980). The Powhatan Renape Nation was a founding member of "CENA" – the Coalition of Eastern Native Americans, with Chief Crazy Horse and Charles Juancito on the Board.

In 1977, Chief Crazy Horse was asked to sit on the American Indian Task Force of President Jimmy Carter's Committee on Mental Health.

Powhatan Leaders 1972

(Left to Right) Chief Oliver Adkins - Chickahommony, Clifton Holmes - Chickahommoy, Mrs. Custalow - Mattoponi, Chief OT Custalow - Mattoponi, Dennis Hoag Bradby - Eastern Chickahommoy, Leon Custalow - Pamunkey, Beulah Tapposcott - Rappahanock, Roy Crazy Horse - Rappahanock, Chief Miles - Pamunkey, Jack Forbes - Rappahanock, Charles Juancito - Rappahanock.

1980: Recognition by the State of New Jersey

In 1980, the State of New Jersey, by Resolution of its Senate, with the concurrence of the General Assembly, recognized the Powhatan Renape Nation. The resolution also called upon the Congress of the United States to recognize the Powhatan Renape Nation. Noting "that these people have an unbroken history of hundreds of years of settlement along the coastal areas of the mid-Atlantic from Virginia north to southern New Jersey, it was resolved:

...that the Powhatan Renape People of the Delaware Valley as the surviving tribes of the Renape linguistic group of the Powhatan alliance, are hereby designated by the State of New Jersey as the Powhatan Renape Nation."

In 1982, the Powhatan Renape Nation negotiated an agreement with the State of New Jersey to take over 350 acres of state-owned land in the town of Westampton. The property is now recognized by the State of New Jersey and the general public as the Rankokus Indian Reservation. Thousands of school children visit it annually to tour its museum, art gallery and the

Governor Thomas Kean with Chief Roy Crazy Horse and community members at the American Indian Arts Festival, Rankokus Indian Reservation, 1985.

Left to Right: Billy King, Curtis Diggs, Marion Hardy, Vernon Johnson, Gilbert Samuels, Richard Brown, Edgar Harmon, Governor Thomas Kean, Gig Schmidt, Floyd Adams, Chief Roy Crazy Horse.

many animal exhibits and nature trails on the grounds. Annual events such as the Indian Arts Festival, the largest of its kind east of the Mississippi River, are held at the Reservation. The Nation's administrative center is located here to manage its community, educational, cultural, social and other programs and services. As such, the Reservation serves as a focal point not only of the Powhatan Renape Nation, but also for American Indians of other nations located in the region.

The spiritual roots of the community, however, remained at Morrisville. By the 1990's, the Powhatan Renape Nation population of "Morrisville," now Delair, occupied 42 separate residences. Many people still live in the same homes that they or their parents built on the lots purchased in the 1920's. Additional members of the Nation lived in the Camden-Philadelphia vicinity. St. Matthew church, founded by Nehemiah Carney, remains a focal point still today.

The leadership shown by tribal chairmen Carl Major, Oklahoma Bradby, Floyd Adams, Kenova Bradby and Chief Crazy Horse has enabled the Powhatan Renape Nation not only to survive, but also to prosper.

Over 400 years of European domination and living in poverty has had devastating effects on culture. Still, the Powhatan people have managed to retain many cultural attributes, particularly those which are demonstrated in strong social relationships with each other.

Former Tribal Chairmen with Powhatan Community Members: Oklahoma Bradby (holding award with Chief Roy Crazy Horse), Kenova Bradby (2nd from right), Carl Major (far right).

Tribal Council and Council of Elders

Clarence & Mary Hunter's House - Purchased 1915, built in 1861 - Morrisville, NJ
Purchased 1993 - Kim T. Hunter

Semi-Annual Juried Art Festivals held each year on the Rankokus Indian Reservation

(Chairman Floyd Adams), Chief Roy Crazy Horse, Wayne Newton, Powhatan Community and Tribal Council Members watching ceremony at Rankokus Indian Reservation

INDEX